for Adven

SACRED
SPACE

for Advent and the Christmas Season 2015–16

SACRED SPACE

November 29, 2015, to January 3, 2016

from the website www.sacredspace.ie

Prayer from the Irish Jesuits

LOYOLA PRESS.
A JESUIT MINISTRY

Chicago

LOYOLA PRESS.
A JESUIT MINISTRY

3441 N. Ashland Avenue
Chicago, Illinois 60657
(800) 621-1008
www.loyolapress.com

Scripture quotations are from *New Revised Standard Version Bible: Catholic Edition*, copyright © 1989, 1993 National Council of the Churches of Christ in the United States of America. Used by permission. All rights reserved.

Advent retreat by Paul Nicholson, SJ, used with permission.

Cover art credit: © iStock/Qweek

ISBN-13: 978-0-8294-4368-4
ISBN-10: 0-8294-4368-1
Library of Congress Control Number: 2015942967

15 16 17 18 19 20 Versa 10 9 8 7 6 5 4 3 2 1

Contents

The Presence of God

Bless all who worship you, almighty God,
from the rising of the sun to its setting:
from your goodness enrich us,
by your love inspire us,
by your Spirit guide us,
by your power protect us,
in your mercy receive us,
now and always.

How to Use This Booklet

During each week of Advent, begin by reading the "Something to think and pray about each day this week." Then go through "The Presence of God," "Freedom," and "Consciousness" steps to help you prepare yourself to hear the Word of God speaking to you. In the next step, "The Word," turn to the Scripture reading for each day of the week. Inspiration points are provided if you need them. Then return to the "Conversation" and "Conclusion" steps. Follow this process every day of Advent.

The Advent retreat at the back of this book follows a similar structure: an invitation to experience stillness, a Scripture passage and reflection points, and suggestions for prayer; you may find it useful to move and back forth between the daily reflections and the retreat.

November 29—December 5, 2015

Something to think and pray about each day this week:

Imagination and Hope

We used to imagine that, despite the diversity within societies and across the world, we could somehow all achieve safe middle-class ambitions like basic financial security, a wholesome family life, an education for excellence, a fulfilling job with a handsome wage, good health and white teeth, a house in the suburbs, freedom to worship, protection from terrorism, and an environment ready to do our bidding. Now we know that life is not so straightforward. We are not here only to make money, though we need that too. We are not here just to enjoy good health, though we all know what an incredible difference that makes. We are not here solely to live morally good lives, admirable though moral living is. We are here for a project so audacious that something within us finds it hard to believe: we are here to transform ourselves and our world. If we cannot believe this, it is because we have downsized our beliefs. It is our greatness rather than our littleness that intimidates us. But hope can heal us, for hope unsettles us with the passionate unrest that propels us toward great things, and it is imagination that gives us the entrance ticket into the hope-filled world of possibility. We can hope in God, for God is the true fulfillment of everything for which we long and desire. God promises us that the best is yet to come.

The Presence of God
Come to me all you who are burdened and I will give you rest.
Here I am, Lord. I come to seek your presence.
I long for your healing power.

Freedom
Lord, grant me the grace to be free from the excesses of this life.
Let me not get caught up with the desire for wealth.
Keep my heart and mind free to love and serve you.

Consciousness
At this moment, Lord, I turn my thoughts to you.
I will leave aside my chores and preoccupations.
I will take rest and refreshment in your presence, Lord.

The Word
The Word of God comes down to us through the Scriptures. May the Holy Spirit enlighten my mind and my heart to respond to the gospel teachings. (Please turn to the Scripture on the following pages.

Inspiration points are there should you need them. When you are ready, return here to continue.)

Conversation
Jesus, you speak to me through the words of the Gospels.
May I respond to your call today.
Teach me to recognize your hand at work in my daily living.

Conclusion
Glory be to the Father, and to the Son, and to the Holy Spirit,
As it was in the beginning, is now and ever shall be, world without end. Amen.

Sunday 29th November
First Sunday of Advent

Luke 21:25–28, 34–36

Jesus said, "There will be signs in the sun, the moon, and the stars, and on the earth distress among nations confused by the roaring of the sea and the waves. People will faint from fear and foreboding of what is coming upon the world, for the powers of the heavens will be shaken. Then they will see 'the Son of Man coming in a cloud' with power and great glory. Now when these things begin to take place, stand up and raise your heads because your redemption is drawing near. Be on guard so that your hearts are not weighed down with dissipation and drunkenness and the worries of this life, and that day does not catch you unexpectedly, like a trap. For it will come upon all who live on the face of the whole earth. Be alert at all times, praying that you may have the strength to escape all these things that will take place, and to stand before the Son of Man."

- Jesus is using traditional Jewish symbolism to describe what will happen when God's final judgment occurs. He says that people will see "the Son of Man coming in a cloud." The cloud is a symbol for God's presence. Jesus' message bursts with hope and confidence because, unlike those who have reason to fear his coming, Jesus' followers will be able to hold their heads high because their liberation is at hand.

• Jesus urges me to be on guard so that my heart is not weighed down by the worries of life. What are the worries and cares of life that weigh me down today? As I prepare for a conversation with Jesus, can I bring my worries and cares to him in prayer?

Monday 30th November
Matthew 4:18–22

As Jesus walked by the Sea of Galilee, he saw two brothers, Simon, who is called Peter, and Andrew his brother, casting a net into the lake—for they were fishermen. And he said to them, "Follow me, and I will make you fish for people." Immediately they left their nets and followed him. As he went from there, he saw two other brothers, James son of Zebedee and his brother John, in the boat with their father Zebedee, mending their nets, and he called them. Immediately they left the boat and their father, and followed him.

• The call of the disciples is rooted in the call of Jesus, and this call is to change their lives forever. The disciples are not only to hear the word of God; they act on it. So the first disciples leave everything and follow him. Jesus will go on to teach the disciples a new way of life, for they cannot be

open to the work of God unless they have their
ears opened by his word.

- I pray: "Jesus, show me what I need to leave behind in order to be a good disciple. Do not let me
fall far behind you and lose sight of you. Keep me
close. Thank you for these times of prayer, and
for inviting me to share a meal with you in the
Eucharist."

Tuesday 1st December
Luke 10:21–24

Jesus rejoiced in the Holy Spirit and said, "I thank
you, Father, Lord of heaven and earth, because you
have hidden these things from the wise and the intel-
ligent and have revealed them to infants; yes, Father,
for such was your gracious will. All things have been
handed over to me by my Father; and no one knows
who the Son is except the Father, or who the Father is
except the Son and anyone to whom the Son chooses
to reveal him." Then turning to the disciples, Jesus
said to them privately, "Blessed are the eyes that see
what you see! For I tell you that many prophets and
kings desired to see what you see, but did not see it,
and to hear what you hear, but did not hear it."

- To rejoice in the Holy Spirit is to be aware of the
Father's infinite and unconditional love poured
out on me. Are there moments in my life when I

have felt such love? What may be preventing me from experiencing such love today?

- How blessed are we to see Jesus and to hear his words! And Jesus has chosen to reveal his Father to us! I consider how this message might make me glad and grateful.

Wednesday 2nd December
Matthew 15:29–37

Jesus passed along the Sea of Galilee, and he went up the mountain, where he sat down. Great crowds came to him, bringing with them the lame, the maimed, the blind, the mute, and many others. They put them at his feet, and he cured them, so that the crowd was amazed when they saw the mute speaking, the maimed whole, the lame walking, and the blind seeing. And they praised the God of Israel. Then Jesus called his disciples to him and said, "I have compassion for the crowd, because they have been with me now for three days and have nothing to eat; and I do not want to send them away hungry, for they might faint on the way." Jesus asked them, "How many loaves have you?" They said, "Seven, and a few small fish." Then ordering the crowd to sit down on the ground, he took the seven loaves and the fish; and after giving thanks he broke them and gave them to the disciples, and the disciples gave them to the crowds.

And all of them ate and were filled; and they took up the broken pieces left over, seven baskets full.

- I imagine the crowd, with everyone bringing their problems to Jesus. The people who approach him have an illness or are accompanying a person with an illness. What problem might I bring, and how does Jesus deal with it? Is this how I deal with the problems others bring to me?

- Jesus takes in the bigger picture: He is in touch with our basic human need for nourishment. What joy he must have had in providing this party in the wilderness! Everything is for sharing; how might I be glad to share what I can? What do my bread and fish look like?

Thursday 3rd December
Matthew 7:21, 24–27

Jesus said to the people, "Not everyone who says to me, 'Lord, Lord,' will enter the kingdom of heaven, but only one who does the will of my Father in heaven. Everyone then who hears these words of mine and acts on them will be like a wise man who built his house on rock. The rain fell, the floods came, and the winds blew and beat on that house, but it did not fall, because it had been founded on rock. And everyone who hears these words of mine and does not act on them will be like a foolish man who built his house on sand. The rain fell, and the floods came, and the winds blew and beat against that house, and it fell— and great was its fall!"

- There are many ways to "hear" words. They can be just sound, external meaning, like giving information or directions. The Word of God is more like the word of a friend, spoken to the mind and to the heart. Or it is like the words of a caring parent, giving advice or directions out of love. The Word of God gives meaning to life and is spoken always in love. Prayer is giving time to hearing this word on the deepest levels of our heart.

- Lord, you never let me forget that love is shown in deeds, not words or feelings. I could fill notebooks with resolutions and in the end be further from you. As the psychologist William James put it, "A resolution that is a fine flame of feeling allowed to burn itself out without appropriate action, is not merely a lost opportunity, but a bar to future action."

Friday 4th December
Matthew 9:27–31

As Jesus went on his way, two blind men followed him, crying loudly, "Have mercy on us, Son of David!" When he entered the house, the blind men came to him; and Jesus said to them, "Do you believe that I am able to do this?" They said to him,

"Yes, Lord." Then he touched their eyes and said, "According to your faith let it be done to you." And their eyes were opened. Then Jesus sternly ordered them, "See that no one knows of this." But they went away and spread the news about him throughout that district.

- The start of this encounter is in public. There are crowds around Jesus, and the blind men are caught up in the general emotion. They shout at Jesus using a formal title, Son of David, as though he were a powerful messianic figure dispensing health to crowds. Jesus waits until he is inside the house, where he can meet the blind men in person and question their faith.

- I hope I have the faith to call out to Jesus, whom I cannot see, and to follow him into a darkened house. I hope I can answer, "Yes, Lord" to the question, "Do you believe that I am able to do this?" and mean it.

Saturday 5th December
Matthew 9:35—10:1, 5a, 6–8

Jesus went about all the cities and villages, teaching in their synagogues, and proclaiming the good news of the kingdom, and curing every disease and every sickness. When he saw the crowds, he had compassion for them, because they were harassed and helpless, like sheep without a shepherd. Then he said to his disciples, "The harvest is plentiful, but the laborers are few; therefore ask the Lord of the harvest to send out laborers into his harvest." Then Jesus summoned his twelve disciples and gave them authority over unclean spirits, to cast them out, and to cure every disease and every sickness. These twelve Jesus sent out with the following instructions: "Go to the lost sheep of the house of Israel. As you go, proclaim the good news, 'The kingdom of heaven has come near.' Cure the sick, raise the dead, cleanse the lepers, cast out demons. You received without payment; give without payment."

- Do I know any people who are harassed and helpless like sheep without a shepherd? Let me hold them before my mind's eye for a moment. Can I now imagine Jesus looking at them? How does he see them?

- There is so much good that is not noticed, so many blessings that are unacknowledged. I pray for a deeper appreciation of the rich harvest that is around me.

The Second Week of Advent
December 6—December 12

Something to think and pray about each day this week:

Endings and Beginnings

There's something at this time of the year about endings and beginnings. An old year is coming to an end with its memories, and a new year will soon begin with its hope. The endings and the beginnings—past and future—are always in the present tense of love. Isn't that where prayer comes in? There are moments in the day—or in the night—in which we immerse ourselves in this mystery of the divine love for us. This love brings healing of the past and trust for the future. All religion worth its name surrounds the past with a wide healing and the possibility of forgiveness and enlightens the future with the same breadth of hope and trust. No matter what our prayer and its content, its context is of healing and trust in the space of a love so large that it is the name given to God. What I live in the ordinariness of the day also forms a context for prayer, and what I experience or think of in prayer forms a context for my life. Neither is separate from the other. Everything that this annual transition of the years evokes in me, I bring to the One who is love beyond all telling.

The Presence of God

The more we call on God, the more we can feel God's presence.

Day by day we are drawn closer to the loving heart of God.

Freedom

God is not foreign to my freedom.

Instead, the Spirit breathes life into my most intimate desires, gently nudging me toward all that is good.

I ask for the grace to let myself be enfolded by the Spirit.

Consciousness

How do I find myself today?

Where am I with God? With others?

Do I have something to be grateful for? Then I give thanks.

Is there something I am sorry for? Then I ask forgiveness.

The Word

I take my time to read the Word of God, slowly, a few times, allowing myself to dwell on anything that strikes me. (Please turn to the Scripture on the following pages. Inspiration points are there should you need them. When you are ready, return here to continue.)

Conversation

How has God's Word moved me? Has it left me cold?
Has it consoled me or moved me to act in a new way?
I imagine Jesus standing or sitting beside me.
I turn and share my feelings with him.

Conclusion

I thank God for these few moments we have spent
alone together and for any insights I may have been
given concerning the text.

Sunday 6th December
Second Sunday of Advent

Luke 3:1–6

In the fifteenth year of the reign of Emperor Tiberius, when Pontius Pilate was governor of Judea, and Herod was ruler of Galilee, and his brother Philip ruler of the region of Ituraea and Trachonitis, and Lysanias ruler of Abilene, during the high priesthood of Annas and Caiaphas, the word of God came to John son of Zechariah in the wilderness. He went into all the region around the Jordan, proclaiming a baptism of repentance for the forgiveness of sins, as it is written in the book of the words of the prophet Isaiah, "The voice of one crying out in the wilderness: 'Prepare the way of the Lord, make his paths straight. Every valley shall be filled, and every mountain and hill shall be made low, and the crooked shall be made straight, and the rough ways made smooth; and all flesh shall see the salvation of God.'"

- The Gospel positions John the Baptist in the history of his time, sign-posting the date of God's intervention in human history. It was not a one-off intervention; it continues through everyone who works to prepare the way of the Lord.

- The paths I follow are often crooked, diverting me from my eternal goal. What can I do to make my path to God straight?

Monday 7th December
Luke 5:17–26

One day, while Jesus was teaching, Pharisees and teachers of the law were sitting nearby (they had come from every village of Galilee and Judea and from Jerusalem); and the power of the Lord was with him to heal. Just then some men came, carrying a paralyzed man on a bed. They were trying to bring him in and lay him before Jesus; but finding no way to bring him in because of the crowd, they went up on the roof and let him down with his bed through the tiles into the middle of the crowd in front of Jesus. When he saw their faith, he said, "Friend, your sins are forgiven you." Then the scribes and the Pharisees began to ask themselves, "Who is this who is speaking blasphemies? Who can forgive sins but God alone?" When Jesus perceived their questionings, he answered them, "Why do you raise such questions in your hearts? Which is easier, to say, 'Your sins are forgiven you,' or to say, 'Stand up and walk'? But so that you may know that the Son of Man has authority on earth to forgive sins"—he said to the one who was paralyzed—"I say to you, stand up and take your bed and go to your home." Immediately he stood up before them, picked up what he had been lying on, and went home, glorifying God. Amazement seized all and them, and they glorified God and were filled with awe, saying, "We have seen strange things today."

- Without the help of his determined friends, the paralyzed man could never have made his way to Jesus to be healed. How might I help a friend find healing in Christ?

- Jesus speaks forgiveness to me. I receive the healing that he offers and ask to understand the new life he has in mind for me.

Tuesday 8th December
The Immaculate Conception
of the Blessed Virgin Mary
Luke 1:26–38

In the sixth month the angel Gabriel was sent by God to a town in Galilee called Nazareth, to a virgin engaged to a man whose name was Joseph, of the house of David. The virgin's name was Mary. And he came to her and said, "Greetings, favored one! The Lord is with you." But she was much perplexed by his words and pondered what sort of greeting this might be. The angel said to her, "Do not be afraid, Mary, for you have found favor with God. And now, you will conceive in your womb and bear a son, and you will name him Jesus. He will be great, and will be called the Son of the Most High, and the Lord God will give to him the throne of his ancestor David. He will reign over the house of Jacob forever, and of his kingdom there will be no end." Mary said to the angel, "How can this be, since I am a virgin?" The angel said to her, "The Holy Spirit will come upon you, and the power of the Most High will overshadow you; therefore the child to be born will be holy; he will be called Son of God. And now, your relative Elizabeth in her old age has also conceived a son; and this is the sixth month for her who was said to be barren. For nothing will be impossible with God." Then Mary said, "Here am I, the servant of the Lord; let it be with me according to your word." Then the angel departed from her.

- Mary was prepared to say "Yes" to the direction God had in mind for her. How might I be as perceptive and as humble as she was, ready to notice and respond?

- Repeating a phrase in prayer may make it go deep within us. It's like a favorite piece of music that we can hum over and over again. It is part of us. "I am the servant of the Lord" was such a phrase for Mary, spoken first at one of the biggest moments in her life. In dry times of prayer, a sentence like that can occupy mind and heart and raise us close to God.

Wednesday 9th December
Matthew 11:28–30

Jesus said, "Come to me, all you that are weary and are carrying heavy burdens, and I will give you rest. Take my yoke upon you, and learn from me; for I am gentle and humble in heart, and you will find rest for your souls. For my yoke is easy, and my burden is light."

- A yoke is a wooden or iron frame that joins two oxen for the purpose of pulling a plow or cart. Here, Jesus invites us to share the burden of our worries and fears with him because he is only too willing to help us cope with and manage them. It is an open invitation spoken to us by Jesus, who is forever "gentle and humble in heart."

- Lord, let me share your work. Open my eyes to the burdens borne by others. Open my heart to the pain that cannot be shared, to the fear that cannot be spoken, to those who face darkness alone.

Thursday 10th December
Matthew 11:11–15

Jesus said, "Truly I tell you, among those born of women no one has arisen greater than John the Baptist; yet the least in the kingdom of heaven is greater than he. From the days of John the Baptist until now the kingdom of heaven has suffered violence, and the violent take it by force. For all the prophets and the law prophesied until John came; and if you are willing to accept it, he is Elijah who is to come. Let anyone with ears listen!"

- I ponder what Jesus said about the greatness of John. I think of what Jesus had seen and heard so that I might profit from understanding what he valued. John proclaimed the gospel, allowing his disciples to leave him to follow Jesus. I think of what it might mean to be less so that Jesus might be more.

- Lord, make me a better listener. Empty me of noise and clutter, to hear what needs to be heard. Let me not be afraid of silence because then you can speak to me. "Let anyone with ears listen!" What is Jesus saying to me in this time of meditation?

Friday 11th December
Matthew 11:16–19

Jesus spoke to the crowds, "But to what will I compare this generation? It is like children sitting in the market places and calling to one another, 'We played the flute for you, and you did not dance; we wailed, and you did not mourn.' For John came neither eating nor drinking, and they say, 'He has a demon'; the Son of Man came eating and drinking, and they say, 'Look, a glutton and a drunkard, a friend of tax collectors and sinners!' Yet wisdom is vindicated by her deeds."

- Jesus notices those who sit back and do nothing except judge others. John is too strange while Jesus is too normal for such people. Am I occasionally cynical and critical? Do I disparage the humble efforts of others when they do their best?

- Do I bear faithful witness to Jesus by good deeds? Such deeds may be costly, but the ultimate course of events will reveal that they were wise decisions.

Saturday 12th December
Luke 1:26–38

In the sixth month the angel Gabriel was sent by God to a town in Galilee called Nazareth, to a virgin engaged to a man whose name was Joseph, of the house of David. The virgin's name was Mary. And he came to her and said, "Greetings, favored one! The Lord is with you." But she was much perplexed by his words and pondered what sort of greeting this might be. The angel said to her, "Do not be afraid, Mary, for you have found favor with God. And now, you will conceive in your womb and bear a son, and you will name him Jesus. He will be great, and will be called the Son of the Most High, and the Lord God will give to him the throne of his ancestor David. He will reign over the house of Jacob forever, and of his kingdom there will be no end." Mary said to the angel, "How can this be, since I am a virgin?" The angel said to her, "The Holy Spirit will come upon you, and the power of the Most High will overshadow you; therefore the child to be born will be holy; he will be called Son of God. And now, your relative Elizabeth in her old age has also conceived a son; and this is the sixth month for her who was said to be barren. For nothing will be impossible with God." Then Mary said, "Here am I, the servant of the Lord; let it be with me according to your word." Then the angel departed from her.

- How does Mary react in a crisis? She hears God's messenger but wonders, Can it be true? And how does it square with my virginity? She knows that she is free to say "Yes" or "No," and her response is from a full heart.

- Lord, this is not an easy prayer to make. You prayed it yourself in Gethsemane in a sweat of blood: "Not my will but yours be done." Help me make it the pattern of my life. What issues of surrender and trust does it raise for me?

December 13—December 19

Something to think and pray about each day this week:

Touching the Flesh of Christ

The ecclesial community is a place to grow our faith. Pope Francis often urges Christians not to lose confidence in the Church, despite its obvious failings. It makes mistakes and clearly needs institutional reform, and this is a major task for the Holy Spirit. But the Church will be chiefly reformed by dedicating itself to its central mission. This means that it must move "to the periphery" and proclaim the Good News to all people from the standpoint of solidarity with the poor. In an address to families, Pope Benedict XVI stressed that Christian charity is best understood in terms of "self-gift." Only in self-giving, he said, do we find ourselves. We must open ourselves to the ecclesial community and to the world. We cannot turn our backs on our struggling sisters and brothers. In the words of Pope Francis, we are to "touch the flesh of Christ" by caring for the needy. The Church is meant to be a servant of all in need. This is a humble role. According to the Second Vatican Council, whatever promotes human dignity among the people of the world becomes the agenda of the Church. Injustice anywhere must stir the Christian heart to an appropriate response.

The Presence of God
Dear Jesus, as I call on you today, I realize that I often come asking for favors.
Today I'd like just to be in your presence.
Let my heart respond to your love.

Freedom
If God were trying to tell me something, would I know?
If God were reassuring me or challenging me, would I notice?
I ask for the grace to be free of my own preoccupations and open to what God may be saying to me.

Consciousness
Help me, Lord, to be more conscious of your presence.
Teach me to recognize your presence in others.
Fill my heart with gratitude for the times your love has been shown to me through the care of others.

The Word
I read the Word of God slowly, a few times over, and I listen to what God is saying to me. (Please turn to the Scripture on the following pages. Inspiration points

are there should you need them. When you are ready, return here to continue.)

Conversation

What feelings are rising in me as I pray and reflect on God's Word?

I imagine Jesus himself sitting or standing near me and open my heart to him.

Conclusion

Glory be to the Father, and to the Son, and to the Holy Spirit,

As it was in the beginning, is now and ever shall be, world without end. Amen.

Sunday 13th December
Third Sunday of Advent

Luke 3:10–18

The crowds asked John the Baptist, "What then should we do?" In reply he said to them, "Whoever has two coats must share with anyone who has none; and whoever has food must do likewise." Even tax collectors came to be baptized, and they asked him, "Teacher, what should we do?" He said to them, "Collect no more than the amount prescribed for you." Soldiers also asked him, "And we, what should we do?" He said to them, "Do not extort money from anyone by threats or false accusation, and be satisfied with your wages." As the people were filled with expectation, and all were questioning in their hearts concerning John, whether he might be the Messiah, John answered all of them by saying, "I baptize you with water; but one who is more powerful than I is coming; I am not worthy to untie the thong of his sandals. He will baptize you with the Holy Spirit and fire. His winnowing fork is in his hand, to clear his threshing floor and to gather the wheat into his granary; but the chaff he will burn with unquenchable fire." So, with many other exhortations, he proclaimed the good news to the people.

- For all the austerity of his life, John the Baptist spoke to people in words they could grasp. It was his austerity that drew people's respect and trust. Here was a man who cared nothing for comfort, money, or fame, who could not be bought, and who could speak the truth without fear.

• What does my lifestyle say about my faith in Christ? Do I hoard or share what I have with others, especially those who are poor and on the margins of society?

Monday 14th December
Matthew 21:23–27

When Jesus entered the temple, the chief priests and the elders of the people came to him as he was teaching, and said, "By what authority are you doing these things, and who gave you this authority?" Jesus said to them, "I will also ask you one question; if you tell me the answer, then I will also tell you by what authority I do these things. Did the baptism of John come from heaven, or was it of human origin?" And they argued with one another, "If we say, 'From heaven,' he will say to us, 'Why then did you not believe him?' But if we say, 'Of human origin,' we are afraid of the crowd; for all regard John as a prophet." So they answered Jesus, "We do not know." And he said to them, "Neither will I tell you by what authority I am doing these things."

- What authority does Jesus have? If he turned up today, would we want to see his qualifications before allowing him to preach? Or would his attitude, words, and deeds resonate deeply within us, so that we would say, "All that he says and does, and the way he does it, is just right"?

- God is busy in our world, trying to get people to see clearly. Like the priests and elders, do I sometimes evade the truth of what God is trying to tell me? I ask Jesus to help me be a truthful person. Even small lies and deceptions should have no place in my speech.

Tuesday 15th December

Matthew 21:28–32

Jesus said, "What do you think? A man had two sons; he went to the first and said, 'Son, go and work in the vineyard today.' He answered, 'I will not'; but later he changed his mind and went. The father went to the second and said the same; and he answered, 'I go, sir'; but he did not go. Which of the two did the will of his father?" They said, "The first." Jesus said to them, "Truly I tell you, the tax collectors and the prostitutes are going into the kingdom of God ahead of you. For John came to you in the way of righteousness and you did not believe him, but the tax collectors and the prostitutes believed him; and even after you saw it, you did not change your minds and believe him."

- Jesus asks us to think about whether our words and actions are in agreement. It is easy to talk—to pronounce and to make statements. It is more difficult to give time, effort, and attention. I profess my faith not only in Sunday words but also in the time I give to working for the reign of God during the week. Jesus values a few small acts more than many fine words.

- Jesus speaks this parable to me. I avoid applying it to others right now and simply accept Jesus' warmth as he sees how I have served. I listen for his invitation as he shows me where I hold back.

Wednesday 16th December
Luke 7:18b–23

At that time, John summoned two of his disciples and sent them to the Lord to ask, "Are you the one who is to come, or are we to wait for another?" When the men had come to him, they said, "John the Baptist has sent us to you to ask, 'Are you the one who is to come, or are we to wait for another?'" Jesus had just then cured many people of diseases, plagues, and evil spirits, and had given sight to many who were blind. And he answered them, "Go and tell John what you have seen and heard: the blind receive their sight, the lame walk, the lepers are cleansed, the deaf hear, the dead are raised, the poor have good news brought to them. And blessed is anyone who takes no offence at me."

• The readings before Christmas search my heart profoundly. Am I longing for Jesus to come more deeply into my life this Advent? Or am I waiting for God to come in some other form? Would I prefer a different kind of "good news" than the gospel about Jesus?

• Jesus wants to hearten me by pointing my attention to where the Spirit is at work. I review my current concerns with God, asking for light and hope.

Thursday 17th December
Matthew 1:1–17

An account of the genealogy of Jesus the Messiah, the son of David, the son of Abraham. Abraham was the father of Isaac, and Isaac the father of Jacob, and Jacob the father of Judah and his brothers, and Judah the father of Perez and Zerah by Tamar, and Perez the father of Hezron, and Hezron the father of Aram, and Aram the father of Aminadab, and Aminadab the father of Nahshon, and Nahshon the father of Salmon, and Salmon the father of Boaz by Rahab, and Boaz the father of Obed by Ruth, and Obed the father of Jesse, and Jesse the father of King David. And David was the father of Solomon by the wife of Uriah, and Solomon the father of Rehoboam, and Rehoboam the father of Abijah, and Abijah the father of Asaph, and Asaph the father of Jehoshaphat, and Jehoshaphat the father of Joram, and Joram the father of Uzziah, and Uzziah the father of Jotham, and Jotham the father of Ahaz, and Ahaz the father of Hezekiah, and Hezekiah the father of Manasseh, and Manasseh the father of Amos, and Amos the father of Josiah, and Josiah the father of Jechoniah and his brothers, at the time of the deportation to Babylon. And after the deportation to Babylon: Jechoniah was the father of Salathiel, and Salathiel the father of Zerubbabel, and Zerubbabel the father of Abiud, and Abiud the father of Eliakim, and Eliakim the father of Azor, and Azor the father of Zadok, and Zadok the father of Achim, and Achim the father of Eliud, and Eliud the father of Eleazar, and Eleazar the father of Matthan, and Matthan the father of Jacob, and Jacob the father of Joseph the husband of Mary, of whom Jesus was born, who is called the Messiah. So all the generations from Abraham to David are fourteen generations; and from David to the deportation to Babylon, fourteen generations; and from the deportation to Babylon to the Messiah, fourteen generations.

- Jesus' family tree is a colorful one. It includes a murderer and an adulterer, Jews and Gentiles, the famous and the nobodies. The powerful and the powerless find a place. So do females and males in odd relationships, as well as the upright and the good. All human life is here, to show that God includes everyone in divine planning. I marvel at this.

- Everyone in human history influences others. I think of people who have influenced me for good or for ill. Then I ask that through my prayer and my life I may be a good influence on others. With Jesus I reflect on my relationships.

Friday 18th December
Matthew 1:18–25

Now the birth of Jesus the Messiah took place in this way. When his mother Mary had been engaged to Joseph, but before they lived together, she was found to be with child from the Holy Spirit. Her husband Joseph, being a righteous man and unwilling to expose her to public disgrace, planned to dismiss her quietly. But just when he had resolved to do this, an angel of the Lord appeared to him in a dream and said, "Joseph, son of David, do not be afraid to take Mary as your wife, for the child conceived in her is from the Holy Spirit. She will bear a son, and you are to name him Jesus, for he will save his people from their sins." All this took place to fulfill what had been spoken by the Lord through the prophet: "Look, the virgin shall conceive and bear a son, and they shall name him Emmanuel," which means, "God is with us." When Joseph awoke from sleep, he did as the angel of the Lord commanded him; he took her as his wife but had no marital relations with her until she had borne a son, and he named him Jesus.

- Joseph is being taught a lesson about the surprising ways in which God works. Surely God is saying something here about the divine ability to bring good even out of situations the world thinks scandalous! "Nothing will be impossible with God."

- Emmanuel: "God is with us." There is never an instant when he is not with me. With him, I shape my own soul every day of my earthly life. I need have no fear of the changes of life. Instead, I see them for what they are: surprising stages along my journey home with him.

Saturday 19th December
Luke 1:5–25

In the days of King Herod of Judea, there was a priest named Zechariah, who belonged to the priestly order of Abijah. His wife was a descendant of Aaron, and her name was Elizabeth. Both of them were righteous before God, living blamelessly according to all the commandments and regulations of the Lord. But they had no children, because Elizabeth was barren, and both were getting on in years. Once when he was serving as priest before God and his section was on duty, he was chosen by lot, according to the custom of the priesthood, to enter the sanctuary of the Lord and offer incense. Now at the time of the incense-offering, the whole assembly of the people was praying outside. Then there appeared to him an angel of the Lord, standing at the right side of the altar of incense. When Zechariah saw him, he was terrified; and fear overwhelmed him. But the angel said to him, "Do not be afraid, Zechariah, for your prayer has been heard. Your wife Elizabeth will bear you a son, and you will name him John. You will have joy and gladness, and many will rejoice at his birth, for he will be great in the sight of the Lord. He must never drink wine or strong drink; even before his birth he will be filled with the Holy Spirit. He will turn many of the people of Israel to the Lord their God. With the spirit and power of Elijah, he will go before him, to turn the hearts of parents to their children, and the disobedient to the wisdom of the righteous, to make ready a people prepared for the Lord." Zechariah said to the angel, "How will I know that this is so? For I am an old man, and my wife is getting on in years." The angel replied, "I am Gabriel. I stand in the presence of God, and I have been sent to speak to you and to bring you this good news. But now, because you did not believe my words, which will be fulfilled in their time, you will become mute, unable to speak, until the day these things occur." Meanwhile, the people were waiting for Zechariah, and wondered at his delay in the sanctuary. When he did come out, he could not speak to them, and they realized that he had seen a vision in the sanctuary. He kept motioning to them and remained unable to speak. When his time of service was ended, he went to his home. After those days his wife Elizabeth conceived, and for five months she remained in seclusion. She said, "This is what the Lord has done for me when he looked favorably on me and took away the disgrace I have endured among my people."

- Zechariah, you lived a dedicated and blameless life. You served on that day as a priest before God, as on any other day. You attended scrupulously to the rites of purification. But nothing prepared you for a direct encounter with God. You never thought that your hope would be answered. Am I a bit like you?

- How much do we live life by simply doing what needs to be done or what is expected of us? Can we own our lives more, claiming the grace of the moment? Can we address our God as if we know that God can hear us? Can we love our dear ones as if we might never see them again? Poor Zechariah, if given a second chance, might have hugged the angel because the encounter promised him "joy and gladness."

December 20—December 26

Something to think and pray about each day this week:

Meeting God Within

When people succeed in coming home to themselves and glimpsing their own inner beauty, something amazing happens: they are blessed with a real compassion for who they themselves are, in all their vulnerabilities. This compassion in turn carves out a space where they can welcome God into their hearts. It is as if they must first become aware of the marvel of themselves, and only then are they ready to get in touch with the wonder of God. Their new relationship with themselves ushers in a nourishing friendship with the One who has always been calling them. This journey inward does not take place overnight. Although the heart is only fifteen inches from the head, it can take us years to arrive at our emotional core. I used to imagine that God didn't particularly like the world because it wasn't spiritual enough. Only later did it dawn on me that God had created the world in love and had passionately left clues to this fact everywhere. The persons and events of my daily life were already signs of God. Had I paid compassionate attention to my longings and my joys, I would have heard in them the symphony of God's own infinite joy. To find God, I did not have to leave the world, but come home to it—and to myself—and God would be there, waiting for me.

The Presence of God
God is with me, but more, God is within me.
Let me dwell for a moment on God's life-giving presence
in my body, in my mind, in my heart,
as I sit here, right now.

Freedom
There are very few people
who realize what God would make of them
if they abandoned themselves into his hands
and let themselves be formed by his grace (Saint Ignatius of Loyola).
I ask for the grace to trust myself totally to God's love.

Consciousness
I exist in a web of relationships—links to nature, people, God.
I trace out these links, giving thanks for the life that flows through them.
Some links are twisted or broken: I may feel regret, anger, disappointment.
I pray for the gift of acceptance and forgiveness.

The Word

God speaks to each one of us individually. I listen attentively to hear what he is saying to me. Read the text a few times, then listen. (Please turn to the Scripture on the following pages. Inspiration points are there should you need them. When you are ready, return here to continue.)

Conversation

Begin to talk to Jesus about the passage of Scripture you have just read. What part of it strikes a chord in you? Perhaps the words of a friend—or some story you have heard recently—will slowly rise to the surface of your consciousness. If so, does the story throw light on what the Scripture passage may be trying to say to you?

Conclusion

I thank God for these few moments we have spent alone together and for any insights I may have been given concerning the text.

Sunday 20th December
Fourth Sunday of Advent
Luke 1:39–45

In those days Mary set out and went with haste to a Judean town in the hill country, where she entered the house of Zechariah and greeted Elizabeth. When Elizabeth heard Mary's greeting, the child leaped in her womb. And Elizabeth was filled with the Holy Spirit and exclaimed with a loud cry, "Blessed are you among women, and blessed is the fruit of your womb. And why has this happened to me, that the mother of my Lord comes to me? For as soon as I heard the sound of your greeting, the child in my womb leaped for joy. And blessed is she who believed that there would be a fulfillment of what was spoken to her by the Lord."

- Elizabeth is given the special grace of an intimate insight and appreciation of what is happening and who is really present. Do I always appreciate what is happening and who is really present?

- When I encounter someone for the first time, do I perceive and respect that person as a son or daughter of God? What about the people I meet on a day-to-day basis?

Monday 21st December

Luke 1:39–45

In those days Mary set out and went with haste to a Judean town in the hill country, where she entered the house of Zechariah and greeted Elizabeth. When Elizabeth heard Mary's greeting, the child leaped in her womb. And Elizabeth was filled with the Holy Spirit and exclaimed with a loud cry, "Blessed are you among women, and blessed is the fruit of your womb. And why has this happened to me, that the mother of my Lord comes to me? For as soon as I heard the sound of your greeting, the child in my womb leaped for joy. And blessed is she who believed that there would be a fulfillment of what was spoken to her by the Lord."

- Elizabeth is the first to bear witness to the Lord's presence in our world. We can bear witness and encourage one another along the way. Helping another to notice God brings hope and consolation way beyond our expectation.

- The Spirit of God in Elizabeth rejoiced in the presence of Mary. I pray for those who have been friends to me, for all whose companionship or example lift my heart.

Tuesday 22nd December
Luke 1:46–56

And Mary said, "My soul magnifies the Lord, and my spirit rejoices in God my Savior, for he has looked with favor on the lowliness of his servant. Surely, from now on all generations will call me blessed; for the Mighty One has done great things for me, and holy is his name. His mercy is for those who fear him from generation to generation. He has shown strength with his arm; he has scattered the proud in the thoughts of their hearts. He has brought down the powerful from their thrones, and lifted up the lowly; he has filled the hungry with good things, and sent the rich away empty. He has helped his servant Israel, in remembrance of his mercy, according to the promise he made to our ancestors, to Abraham and to his descendants forever." And Mary remained with Elizabeth about three months and then returned to her home.

- This glorious prayer, the *Magnificat*, is charged with dynamite. It points to a society in which nobody wants to have too much while others have too little. The hungry are fed and the lowly are raised up.

- Lord, give me Mary's confidence and generosity of spirit. I ask not only to listen to your voice and do your will, but to do it joyfully and fearlessly. Let me answer your call with an exultant "Yes!" because I know that my journey into the unknown will be made radiant by your transfiguring presence.

Wednesday 23rd December
Luke 1:57–66

Now the time came for Elizabeth to give birth, and she bore a son. Her neighbors and relatives heard that the Lord had shown his great mercy to her, and they rejoiced with her. On the eighth day they came to circumcise the child, and they were going to name him Zechariah after his father. But his mother said, "No; he is to be called John." They said to her, "None of your relatives has this name." Then they began motioning to his father to find out what name he wanted to give him. He asked for a writing tablet and wrote, "His name is John." And all of them were amazed. Immediately his mouth was opened and his tongue freed, and he began to speak, praising God. Fear came over all their neighbors, and all these things were talked about throughout the entire hill country of Judea. All who heard them pondered them and said, "What then will this child become?" For, indeed, the hand of the Lord was with him.

• I join in the excitement around the birth of Elizabeth's baby. I become aware that God is fulfilling his plans through human beings who collaborate. So, too, God wants the child to be called John, and this is what happens. In Luke's understanding of salvation, what God decides will eventually be fulfilled. I ask for faith to believe this and to be free of anxiety.

- How do I stay open to the God of Surprises, to the Spirit that moves at will? Is my comfort zone too well defended for me to be surprised by grace?

Thursday 24th December
Luke 1:67–79

His father Zechariah was filled with the Holy Spirit and spoke this prophecy: "Blessed be the Lord God of Israel, for he has looked favorably on his people and redeemed them. He has raised up a mighty savior for us in the house of his servant David, as he spoke through the mouth of his holy prophets from of old, that we would be saved from our enemies and from the hand of all who hate us. Thus he has shown the mercy promised to our ancestors, and has remembered his holy covenant, the oath that he swore to our ancestor Abraham, to grant us that we, being rescued from the hands of our enemies, might serve him without fear, in holiness and righteousness before him all our days. And you, child, will be called the prophet of the Most High; for you will go before the Lord to prepare his ways, to give knowledge of salvation to his people by the forgiveness of their sins. By the tender mercy of our God, the dawn from on high will break upon us, to give light to those who sit in darkness and in the shadow of death, to guide our feet into the way of peace."

- The *Benedictus* is a prayer of prophecy about the coming of the Savior. This "Most High" that Zechariah mentions comes not in a cloud of glory, but as a vulnerable child, with an ordinary family, in a cold stable. That is the kind of God we have.

- The prayer of Zechariah is a morning prayer for thousands every day. I read it slowly, letting the words reveal their meaning for me today.

Friday 25th December
The Nativity of the Lord

John 1:1–18

In the beginning was the Word, and the Word was with God, and the Word was God. He was in the beginning with God. All things came into being through him, and without him not one thing came into being. What has come into being in him was life, and the life was the light of all people. The light shines in the darkness, and the darkness did not overcome it. There was a man sent from God, whose name was John. He came as a witness to testify to the light, so that all might believe through him. He himself was not the light, but he came to testify to the light. The true light, which enlightens everyone, was coming into the world. He was in the world, and the world came into being through him; yet the world did not know him. He came to what was his own, and his own people did not accept him. But to all who received him, who believed in his name, he gave power to become children of God, who were born, not of blood or of the will of the flesh or of the will of man, but of God. And the Word became flesh and lived among us, and we have seen his glory, the glory as of a father's only son, full of grace and truth. (John testified to him and cried out, "This was he of whom I said, 'He who comes after me ranks ahead of me because he was before me.'") From his fullness we have all received, grace upon grace. The law indeed was given through Moses; grace and truth came through Jesus Christ. No one has ever seen God. It is God the only Son, who is close to the Father's heart, who has made him known.

- The Light of the World has come among us. He is born in the night, with his own star blazing above him. He lies in the dimness of a stable, that same Lord who, as a pillar of cloud by day and a pillar of fire by night, led the Israelites to freedom. He has come to bring his people from darkness into light. As we gaze into the manger, at the tiny creature who is given to us as a light to the nations, we can only whisper, "Come, let us adore him."

- Now that Jesus has arrived, I have a whole new meaning to my life. I am becoming a daughter or son of God! I have been adopted into God's own family. I am important to God! I can now feel happy about myself, no matter what difficulties may be in my life. Everyone else is important, too, so I ask to have great reverence from now on, for myself and for those around me.

Saturday 26th December
Matthew 10:17–22

Jesus said to his disciples, "Beware of them, for they will hand you over to councils and flog you in their synagogues; and you will be dragged before governors and kings because of me, as a testimony to them and the Gentiles. When they hand you over, do not worry about how you are to speak or what you are to say; for what you are to say will be given to you at that time; for it is not you who speak, but the Spirit of your Father speaking through you. Brother will betray brother to death, and a father his child, and children will rise against parents and have them put to death; and you will be hated by all because of my name. But the one who endures to the end will be saved."

- It is a shock to read this gospel passage immediately after Christmas. But this is the world into which Jesus comes. He does not retreat from it in fear or disgust. He will wrap it in his love, and that will be enough to save humankind. I ask for Jesus' courage and love.

- Wisdom, it is said, is making peace with the unchangeable. Do I make peace with any suffering that comes my way?

December 27, 2015—January 3, 2016

Something to think and pray about each day this week:

What Shall I Say?

I work with homeless kids. They're tough, but sometimes one whom I have known for years will sit down in front of me and say, "Can I ask you something?" "Sure," I reply. The kid admits he has seriously offended society in some way, then says, "You won't give up on me, will you?" What shall I say? The conviction that everyone is to be loved infinitely and unconditionally is the foundation stone of a commitment to justice. Starting with myself, I believe that I am loved infinitely. What does love mean here? Love means wanting someone's happiness. Every loving parent wants to give their child all the happiness they can. And God, the Great Giver of Gifts, wishes me to have infinite happiness. That is why I can assert that I am loved infinitely. I am also valued beyond price. My value comes from the infinite love that the Giver of the Gifts has for me. So I am of infinite value. Western culture values people by their achievements, by what they do. We look up to those who succeed and look down on those who have not achieved. But if we have living faith, we value people instead by gospel values. I am valued and loved unconditionally.

And so no one, nothing, not even my own sinfulness, can take away the value and dignity that God's love bestows on me.

The Presence of God
Dear Jesus, I come to you today longing for your presence.
I desire to love you as you love me.
May nothing ever separate me from you.

Freedom
In these days, God teaches me as a schoolteacher teaches a pupil (Saint Ignatius of Loyola).
I remind myself that there are things God has to teach me yet and ask for the grace to hear them and let them change me.

Consciousness
Where do I sense hope, encouragement, and growth areas in my life?
By looking back over the last few months, I may be able to see which activities and occasions have produced rich fruit.
If I do notice such areas, I will determine to give those areas both time and space in the future.

The Word
The Word of God comes down to us through the Scriptures. May the Holy Spirit enlighten my mind and my heart to respond to the gospel teachings. (Please turn to the Scripture on the following pages. Inspiration points are there should you need them. When you are ready, return here to continue.)

Conversation
Conversation requires talking and listening.
As I talk to Jesus, may I also learn to be still and listen. I picture the gentleness in his eyes and his smile full of love as he gazes on me.
I can be totally honest with Jesus as I tell him of my worries and my cares.
I will open up my heart to him as I tell him of my fears and my doubts.
I will ask him to help me place myself fully in his care, to abandon myself to him, knowing that he always wants what is best for me.

Conclusion
Glory be to the Father, and to the Son, and to the Holy Spirit,
As it was in the beginning, is now and ever shall be, world without end. Amen.

Sunday 27th December
The Holy Family of Jesus, Mary, and Joseph
Luke 2:41–52

Now every year his parents went to Jerusalem for the festival of the Passover. And when he was twelve years old, they went up as usual for the festival. When the festival was ended and they started to return, the boy Jesus stayed behind in Jerusalem, but his parents did not know it. Assuming that he was in the group of travelers, they went a day's journey. Then they started to look for him among their relatives and friends. When they did not find him, they returned to Jerusalem to search for him. After three days they found him in the temple, sitting among the teachers, listening to them and asking them questions. And all who heard him were amazed at his understanding and his answers. When his parents saw him they were astonished; and his mother said to him, "Child, why have you treated us like this? Look, your father and I have been searching for you in great anxiety." He said to them, "Why were you searching for me? Did you not know that I must be in my Father's house?" But they did not understand what he said to them. Then he went down with them and came to Nazareth, and was obedient to them. His mother treasured all these things in her heart. And Jesus increased in wisdom and in years, and in divine and human favor.

- "In my Father's house." Do I believe that the Father's house may be found within me? If I do, I can perhaps open myself to an even greater wonder: "Those who love me will keep my word, and my Father will love them, and we will come to them and make our home with them" (John 14:23).

- Let me take in this scene slowly. Jesus is coming of age, entering his teens, and is an eager student questioning his teachers. To his mother's query—"Your father and I"—he points gently to another paternity: "I must be in my Father's house." No gospel scene shows more clearly the gradual process by which he grew into a sense of his mission. Let me savor it.

Monday 28th December
Matthew 2:13–18

Now after the wise men had left, an angel of the Lord appeared to Joseph in a dream and said, "Get up, take the child and his mother, and flee to Egypt, and remain there until I tell you; for Herod is about to search for the child, to destroy him." Then Joseph got up, took the child and his mother by night, and went to Egypt, and remained there until the death of Herod. This was to fulfill what had been spoken by the Lord through the prophet, "Out of Egypt I have called my son." When Herod saw that he had been tricked by the wise men, he was infuriated, and he sent and killed all the children in and around Bethlehem who were two years old or under, according to the time that he had learned from the wise men. Then was fulfilled what had been spoken through the prophet Jeremiah: "A voice was heard in Ramah, wailing and loud lamentation, Rachel weeping for her children; she refused to be consoled, because they are no more."

- There is something about the murder of children that shakes our faith. How could God allow the innocent and unprotected, whose whole lives lie before them, to be killed by evil people? We are driven back to the psalms of rage and protest:

   "Yahweh, how much longer are the wicked to
        triumph?
   Are these evil men to remain unsilenced,
   boasting and asserting themselves?
   No! Yahweh is still my citadel,
   my God is a rock where I take shelter.
   He will pay them back for all their sins,
   he will silence their wickedness,
   Yahweh our God will silence them" (Psalm 94).

- Lord, you have tasted human uncertainties and the difficulties of survival. Your mother, so blissfully happy when she prayed the *Magnificat*, had to adjust rapidly to homelessness and the life of asylum seekers. Let me be equally unsurprisable when you ask me to taste uncertainties and plans going awry.

Tuesday 29th December
Luke 2:22–35

When the time came for their purification according to the law of Moses, they brought him up to Jerusalem to present him to the Lord (as it is written in the law of the Lord, "Every firstborn male shall be designated as holy to the Lord"), and they offered a sacrifice according to what is stated in the law of the Lord, "a pair of turtledoves or two young pigeons." Now there was a man in Jerusalem whose name was Simeon; this man was righteous and devout, looking forward to the consolation of Israel, and the Holy Spirit rested on him. It had been revealed to him by the Holy Spirit that he would not see death before he had seen the Lord's Messiah. Guided by the Spirit, Simeon came into the temple; and when the parents brought in the child Jesus, to do for him what was customary under the law, Simeon took him in his arms and praised God, saying, "Master, now you are dismissing your servant in peace, according to your word; for my eyes have seen your salvation, which you have prepared in the presence of all peoples, a light for revelation to the Gentiles and for glory to your people Israel." And the child's father and mother were amazed at what was being said about him. Then Simeon blessed them and said to his mother Mary, "This child is destined for the falling and the rising of many in Israel, and to be a sign that will be opposed so that the inner thoughts of many will be revealed— and a sword will pierce your own soul too."

- Simeon was one of those known as the "quiet in the land"—Jews who did not look for a military Messiah. He had no dreams of armies or power but believed in a life of constant watchfulness and prayer until God should come. There is a double surprise here: the delight of Simeon at being able to welcome the Promised One and the astonishment of Mary and Joseph at what was being said about their boy.

- I watch Mary carefully handing over Jesus into Simeon's arms. I see the delight on the old man's face. The consolation he had waited for has come. Simeon hands the child back to me, and I ask that I may recognize in Jesus the consolation I need.

Wednesday 30th December
Luke 2:36–40

There was also a prophet, Anna the daughter of Phanuel, of the tribe of Asher. She was of a great age, having lived with her husband seven years after her marriage, then as a widow to the age of eighty-four.

She never left the temple but worshipped there with fasting and prayer night and day. At that moment she came, and began to praise God and to speak about the child to all who were looking for the redemption of Jerusalem. When they had finished everything required by the law of the Lord, they returned to Galilee, to their own town of Nazareth. The child grew and became strong, filled with wisdom; and the favor of God was upon him.

- Anna, another of the "quiet in the land," had lived to a great age. All we know of her is this moment of recognition and blessing. That last sentence summarizes 90 percent of our knowledge of the biography of Jesus, a hidden life as he grew strong and wise. Lord, you are telling me that it is no harm to live quietly and to allow time for your favor to be upon me.

- Mary must have pondered endlessly in her heart about her baby son. He is so ordinary: he eats, sleeps, plays, laughs, and cries. He learns easily; he is a blessed child. But is the angel's promise true, that this is in reality the Son of God? How can it be? And yet there are the crumbs of confirmation: Elizabeth's blessing, the angels and the shepherds, the kings from the east, and now Simeon's and Anna's words. Mary is given enough to help her believe, and so are we.

Thursday 31st December

John 1:1–18

In the beginning was the Word, and the Word was with God, and the Word was God. He was in the beginning with God. All things came into being through him, and without him not one thing came into being. What has come into being in him was life, and the life was the light of all people. The light shines in the darkness, and the darkness did not overcome it. There was a man sent from God, whose name was John. He came as a witness to testify to the light, so that all might believe through him. He himself was not the light, but he came to testify to the light. The true light, which enlightens everyone, was coming into the world. He was in the world, and the world came into being through him; yet the world did not know him. He came to what was his own, and his own people did not accept him. But to all who received him, who believed in his name, he gave power to become children of God, who were born, not of blood or of the will of the flesh or of the will of man, but of God. And the Word became flesh and lived among us, and we have seen his glory, the glory as of a father's only son, full of grace and truth. (John testified to him and cried out, "This was he of whom I said, 'He who comes after me ranks ahead of me because he was before me.'") From his fullness we have all received, grace upon grace. The law indeed was given through Moses; grace and truth came through Jesus Christ. No one has ever seen God. It is God the only Son, who is close to the Father's heart, who has made him known.

- In this hymn that introduces the fourth Gospel, John proclaims the faith that marks us as Christians. We believe that Jesus is the Word of God, his perfect expression. "No one has ever seen God. It is God the only Son, who is close to the Father's heart, who has made him known."

- We often say that it is hard to pray because we cannot imagine God. But God has seen this problem and has painted a perfect self-portrait in Jesus. Now we know what God thinks about us and how much God loves us. I make a New Year's resolution: in the year ahead, I will give quality time to getting to know Jesus better.

Friday 1st January
Solemnity of Mary, the
Holy Mother of God
Luke 2:16–21

So they went with haste and found Mary and Joseph, and the child lying in the manger. When they saw this, they made known what had been told them about this child; and all who heard it were amazed at what the shepherds told them. But Mary treasured all these words and pondered them in her heart. The shepherds returned, glorifying and praising God for all they had heard and seen, as it had been told them. After eight days had passed, it was time to circumcise the child; and he was called Jesus, the name given by the angel before he was conceived in the womb.

- The first day of the New Year is a fresh start in the following of Jesus. We could be anxious, but we are people of a great Promise and so we begin with trust and courage. In Mary's son we have the certain hope that the Word of God made flesh lives among us and takes on himself our fears and our heaviness.

- Lord, like Mary may I find room in my cluttered life simply to rest and be quiet in your presence. Mary's heart was a sacred space, and mine is also. Fill it with the joy of your presence.

Saturday 2nd January

John 1:19–28

This is the testimony given by John when the Jews sent priests and Levites from Jerusalem to ask him, "Who are you?" He confessed and did not deny it, but confessed, "I am not the Messiah." And they asked him, "What then? Are you Elijah?" He said, "I am not." "Are you the prophet?" He answered, "No."

Then they said to him, "Who are you? Let us have an answer for those who sent us. What do you say about yourself?" He said, "I am the voice of one crying out in the wilderness, 'Make straight the way of the Lord,'" as the prophet Isaiah said. Now they had been sent from the Pharisees. They asked him, "Why then are you baptizing if you are neither the Messiah, nor Elijah, nor the prophet?" John answered them, "I baptize with water. Among you stands one whom you do not know, the one who is coming after me; I am not worthy to untie the thong of his sandal." This took place in Bethany across the Jordan where John was baptizing.

- There is a question for me: "Who are you? What do you say about yourself?" Lord, I think of you beside me, seeing the good and the promise in me. This is what I want to say about myself: I am called into being by God, who loves me.

- In prayer God speaks words of comfort and assurance into the wildernesses of our lives—our bad moments of guilt, fear, anxiety, and resentment. God speaks words that help us put ourselves into a bigger world, the world of the love of God. In prayer God also calls each of us to be voices in the wilderness for others in their search for love, for meaning, for faith, and for God.

Sunday 3rd January
The Epiphany of the Lord
Matthew 2:1–12

In the time of King Herod, after Jesus was born in Bethlehem of Judea, wise men from the East came to Jerusalem, asking, "Where is the child who has been born king of the Jews? For we observed his star at its rising, and have come to pay him homage." When King Herod heard this, he was frightened, and all Jerusalem with him; and calling together all the chief priests and scribes of the people, he inquired of them where the Messiah was to be born. They told him, "In Bethlehem of Judea; for so it has been written by the prophet: 'And you, Bethlehem, in the land of Judah, are by no means least among the rulers of Judah; for from you shall come a ruler who is to shepherd my people Israel.'" Then Herod secretly called for the wise men and learned from them the exact time when the star had appeared. Then he sent them to Bethlehem, saying, "Go and search diligently for the child; and when you have found him, bring me word so that I may also go and pay him homage." When they had heard the king, they set out; and there, ahead of them, went the star that they had seen at its rising, until it stopped over the place where the child was. When they saw that the star had stopped, they were overwhelmed with joy. On entering the house, they saw the child with Mary his mother; and they knelt down and paid him homage. Then, opening their treasure-chests, they offered him gifts of gold, frankincense, and myrrh. And having been warned in a dream not to return to Herod, they left for their own country by another road.

- The wise men saw the star and steadily followed it. The people in Jerusalem did not. What star am I being called to follow this year? What gifts from my treasure chest will I offer Jesus in service of his mission? Lord, send me out each day to be a bearer of your love to all I encounter.

- Life is sometimes full of questions, seeking, and searching. I pray that I may always seek the truth and that I might recognize it when God puts it in my path.

An Advent Retreat

Welcome to your Advent retreat. This year we will look at a few of Jesus' ancestors listed in the first chapter of Matthew, to see their role in the unfolding history of our salvation. To begin, it might be worth taking some time to consider where your own faith comes from. Is it something that you can trace back to your parents and grandparents, and perhaps beyond them? Or do you think of your faith as something more personal, owing little or nothing to your family and friends? Notice that neither answer here is better than the other. Each of us owes our faith to other people—even if books brought you to Christianity, you can acknowledge the role of the authors. Yet each of us, too, has to make a personal decision to be a disciple.

Ultimately what is true of Jesus is also true of you. God has been planning to bring you into being since before the world was formed. All through the generations, God has been preparing a place for you in this world, in some particular place or places, and among particular people. As we look over the sessions of this retreat, we pray that we might become more deeply aware of the wise and providential love by which God calls and shapes each one of us.

Consider these points as you begin:

- Decide how long you will devote to each session of the retreat. Each session is designed to last 20–25 minutes.

- Plan which time of day you will pray the retreat.

- Know why you are making the retreat. What gifts and graces do you hope to receive? Begin by asking for the graces you desire.

- Before starting, become aware of God welcoming you to meet him in this way, and be conscious of all those around the world who are praying this retreat alongside you.

Introduction

In recent years, the idea of tracing your ancestry has caught the public imagination. TV shows follow celebrities as they discover their ancestors. Websites help more ordinary people to do the same. Census data takes you so far, but if you want to go further back, you have to do the more difficult work of tracing parish registers with their records of births, marriages and deaths. Often there are surprises, as people find relatives from faraway places or with unlikely professions. Most families have a black sheep or two, but people also uncover accounts of lives lived well in difficult circumstances.

The Gospel of Matthew begins with a chapter tracing the ancestry of Jesus back through forty-two generations! He begins with Abraham, a man the Catholic liturgy calls "our father in faith." It's clearly a carefully structured presentation, and it divides the list into three groups of fourteen. These are interrupted by two of the key events in Jewish religious history: the reign of David, perhaps the greatest of the Jewish kings, and the moment of crisis when the nation's elite was deported to Babylon. Matthew's overall aim is to demonstrate how from the earliest moment of the history of Israel, God's plan to send Jesus, his Son, was being prepared for and worked out.

Matthew traces Jesus' descent through the male line, so the text takes on an almost hypnotic quality. "Abraham was the father of Isaac, and Isaac the father of Jacob, and Jacob the father of Judah . . ." Some of those named are figures well known to biblical history: Abraham, David, Solomon, and Joseph, "the husband of Mary, of whom Jesus was born." Others will be familiar only to those with a good knowledge of the Old Testament: Jesse, King David's father, or Jechoniah, the king deposed and taken into exile in Babylon. A third group is wholly unknown outside of the list that Matthew has drawn up. There are saints and sinners, Jews and the occasional foreigner, and now and then the name of a mother as well as a father.

The foundational Scripture for this retreat is:
Matthew 1:1–17

An account of the genealogy of Jesus the Messiah, the son of David, the son of Abraham.

Abraham was the father of Isaac, and Isaac the father of Jacob, and Jacob the father of Judah and his brothers, and Judah the father of Perez and Zerah by Tamar, and Perez the father of Hezron, and Hezron the father of Aram, and Aram the father of Aminadab, and Aminadab the father of Nahshon, and Nahshon the father of Salmon, and Salmon the father of Boaz by Rahab, and Boaz the father of Obed by Ruth, and Obed the father of Jesse, and Jesse the father of King David.

And David was the father of Solomon by the wife of Uriah, and Solomon the father of Rehoboam, and Rehoboam the father of Abijah, and Abijah the father of Asaph, and Asaph the father of Jehoshaphat, and Jehoshaphat the father of Joram, and Joram the father of Uzziah, and Uzziah the father of Jotham, and Jotham the father of Ahaz, and Ahaz the father of Hezekiah, and Hezekiah the father of Manasseh, and Manasseh the father of Amos, and Amos the father of Josiah, and Josiah the father of Jechoniah and his brothers, at the time of the deportation to Babylon.

And after the deportation to Babylon: Jechoniah was the father of Salathiel, and Salathiel the father of

Zerubbabel, and Zerubbabel the father of Abiud, and Abiud the father of Eliakim, and Eliakim the father of Azor, and Azor the father of Zadok, and Zadok the father of Achim, and Achim the father of Eliud, and Eliud the father of Eleazar, and Eleazar the father of Matthan, and Matthan the father of Jacob, and Jacob the father of Joseph the husband of Mary, of whom Jesus was born, who is called the Messiah.

So all the generations from Abraham to David are fourteen generations; and from David to the deportation to Babylon, fourteen generations; and from the deportation to Babylon to the Messiah, fourteen generations.

Session 1
Invitation

- When you begin a time of prayerful reflection, it's always worth taking a few moments to become more still, more silent, more focused. There are different ways of doing this, and you may already know one that suits you well. As you begin this time of prayer today, pay attention to whatever sounds you can hear around you. You may be in a very quiet place; still, there is likely to be something you can hear. Or there may be a lot of noise around you, all the clamor of everyday life. Whatever your surroundings are like just now, notice the different sounds, and notice, too, where they come from.

Stillness Exercise

- Now bring your attention inward, and concentrate on any sounds nearer to you. Let the others go—they'll still be there in the background. Focus on anything you can hear nearby, in the room where you are or coming from whatever or whoever is close by. Pay attention for a moment to those more immediate sounds.

- Now leave those sounds, in their turn, to fade into the background as you let your attention move inward. Find a quiet place within yourself and, for a moment or two, simply rest there, in the quiet at the center of yourself.

- Hear God's word spoken into that quiet place, as you listen to the account that the book of Genesis gives of God's calling of Abraham.

Scripture
Genesis 12:1–7

Now the LORD said to Abram, "Go from your country and your kindred and your father's house to the land that I will show you. I will make of you a great nation, and I will bless you, and make your name great, so that you will be a blessing. I will bless those who bless you, and the one who curses you I will curse; and in you all the families of the earth shall be blessed."

So Abram went, as the LORD had told him; and Lot went with him. Abram was seventy-five years old when he departed from Haran. Abram took his wife Sarai and his brother's son Lot, and all the possessions that they had gathered, and the persons whom they had acquired in Haran; and they set forth to go to the land of Canaan. When they had come to the land of Canaan, Abram passed through the land to the place at Shechem, to the oak of Moreh. At that time the Canaanites were in the land. Then the LORD appeared to Abram, and said, "To your offspring I will give this land." So he built there an altar to the LORD, who had appeared to him.

Reflect

- Abram, later given the name Abraham by God, is the first name in the list of ancestors of Jesus that Matthew noted in his Gospel. The passage that you have just read is the call that invites him to set out to the Promised Land. It was by answering this call that Abraham became "our father in faith." Where and how did your own faith journey begin?

- Abram, later to take the name "Abraham," sets out because God makes him a promise: "I will make of you a great nation." He puts his trust in God, and in God's faithfulness to him. If you were challenged to account for your faith, to explain why you are, and remain, a Christian, what answer would you give? Are you aware of anything that God has promised you in your own life?

- God's promise is not made to Abraham alone. He sets out with his wife, his nephew, much of his extended family—his entire household. And the promise extends forward: "To your offspring I will give this land." Who are the people who accompany you on your faith journey, who support you and look to you to help them as they try to be Christ's disciples?

Talk to the Lord

- Later in his Gospel, Matthew will tell of Jesus calling the God he knows as Abba—"the God of Abraham, the God of Isaac, and the God of Jacob." Here Abraham is named with his son and his grandson, the first three figures in Jesus' ancestry as Matthew traces it. Through these generations, God's promises are fulfilled. Yet Isaac is not born until Abraham and his wife are already old, and he very nearly becomes a human sacrifice. And Jacob only inherits the promise by tricking his older brother, Esau, out of it. God's promises are, it seems, often fulfilled in unexpected ways, sometimes when people have given up all hope. Can you see times when God has worked like that in your own life?

- At the end of this passage, Abraham, who has reached the Promised Land, builds an altar there to give thanks to God for all that God has done for him. You might like to end today's prayer by taking a few minutes to thank God for some of the good things he has done for you and the promises he has fulfilled in your own life.

Session 2

Invitation

- Begin today's prayer by taking a few moments to move more deeply into quiet by focusing on your own breathing. It's important that you don't try and change its rhythm or depth. All you have to do is notice it. Notice as you breathe in and as you breathe out. Be aware of the air being drawn into your lungs, and then be aware, too, of it being returned to the atmosphere as you breathe out. Simply and calmly, pay attention now to your next half-dozen breaths.

Stillness Exercise

- This time, as you breathe in, let your attention follow your breath into your chest. In Hebrew, the words for "breath" and "spirit," as in the "Holy Spirit," are the same. So imagine breathing in God's breath, God's Spirit, and letting the center of yourself become flooded with the Spirit's warmth and light.

- Now let your breathing continue quietly in the background, and let your attention stay with the Spirit at the heart of yourself, just resting there in that place of quiet stillness.

- And in that place of quiet stillness, pay attention to the word of God as it comes to you now in this passage from the book of Ruth.

Scripture
Ruth 2:8–13

Then Boaz said to Ruth, "Now listen, my daughter, do not go to glean in another field or leave this one, but keep close to my young women. Keep your eyes on the field that is being reaped, and follow behind them. I have ordered the young men not to bother you. If you get thirsty, go to the vessels and drink from what the young men have drawn." Then she fell prostrate, with her face to the ground, and said to him, "Why have I found favor in your sight, that you should take notice of me, when I am a foreigner?" But Boaz answered her, "All that you have done for your mother-in-law since the death of your husband has been fully told me, and how you left your father and mother and your native land and came to a people that you did not know before. May the LORD reward you for your deeds, and may you have a full reward from the LORD, the God of Israel, under whose wings you have come for refuge!" Then she said, "May I continue to find favor in your sight, my lord, for you have comforted me and spoken kindly to your servant, even though I am not one of your servants."

Reflect

- According to the list of the ancestors of Jesus that Matthew offers at the beginning of his Gospel, Boaz and Ruth are the great-grandparents of King David. Ruth is only the second woman that Matthew mentions here. It's all the more surprising, then, that she is a foreigner, not one of the Chosen People at all. She comes originally from Moab, a country on the far side of the Dead Sea from Israel. Are you aware in yourself, or among people you know, of any suspicion toward or distrust of foreigners? Does that give you a sense of how Ruth might have been regarded by the Jews among whom she was living?

- As we join this story, Ruth is a poor widow, caring for her elderly mother-in-law. She is trying to earn a living by gathering grain in the fields of Boaz, a rich nobleman in Jewish society. At first she doesn't realize that she has caught his eye and that he has asked his men to protect her. Can you recall an occasion when you have been on the receiving end of some unexpected kindness? Can that experience help you get a clearer sense of what Ruth is feeling in this passage?

Talk to the Lord

- Boaz has heard how Ruth left her own country, and how, after she was widowed, she cared for her mother-in-law, Naomi. He prays that God will reward and protect her. At the same time, he offers her his own support and, eventually, his love. Their child, Obed, will be the next step on the line leading to Christ. God is shown to be working through the everyday kindness and mutual attraction of these two people to fulfill his plans. Where are you most aware of God working through the everyday events and relationships of your own life?

- As you finish this time of prayer, speak to God for a moment or two about some of the unexpected people who have helped you to come closer to God in your own life. Maybe you could be on the lookout this week for God working through the least likely people around you.

Session 3
Invitation

- The prayer in each session of this retreat invites you to a different way of growing more still, more focused, in preparation for hearing God's word. Today you could begin by picking up some kind of physical object, something that you can comfortably hold. It could be a cup, a piece of fruit, a feather, or a pebble. If there is nothing at hand, you might focus on a piece of clothing that you are wearing. Choose something, and sit quietly for a moment with it.

Stillness Exercise

- Now turn this object over in your hands. Look closely at it. Notice how it feels, how heavy it is, whether it is rough or smooth, hard or soft. Let your whole attention, for a few moments, be focused on this object that you're holding.

Scripture
I Chronicles 28:2, 4–8

Then King David rose to his feet and said: "Hear me, my brothers and my people. I had planned to build a house of rest for the ark of the covenant of the LORD, for the footstool of our God; and I made preparations for building. Yet the LORD God of Israel chose me

from all my ancestral house to be king over Israel forever; for he chose Judah as leader, and in the house of
Judah my father's house, and among my father's sons
he took delight in making me king over all Israel. And
of all my sons, for the Lord has given me many, he
has chosen my son Solomon to sit upon the throne of
the kingdom of the Lord over Israel. He said to me,
"It is your son Solomon who shall build my house and
my courts, for I have chosen him to be a son to me,
and I will be a father to him. I will establish his kingdom forever if he continues resolute in keeping my
commandments and my ordinances, as he is today."
Now therefore in the sight of all Israel, the assembly of
the Lord, and in the hearing of our God, observe and
search out all the commandments of the Lord your
God; that you may possess this good land, and leave it
for an inheritance to your children after you forever."

Reflect

- Of all Jesus' ancestors, the two most illustrious are
  undoubtedly David and Solomon, remembered as
  the greatest kings of Israel. David was a military
  leader, defeating Israel's enemies and establishing
  Jerusalem as the capital. Solomon built the Temple
  at the heart of that city. And, as David reminds the
  people here, they were chosen by God to do these
  things. How do you respond to the idea that you,

too, might have been specially chosen by God to
help him carry out his plans for our world?

- David didn't enjoy an easy life. His predecessor as
  king, Saul, saw him as a rival and tried to kill him.
  Later, several of his sons rose in civil war against
  him. Yet at the end of his life, David could recognize God working through all these experiences,
  those that seemed good and those that seemed
  bad. Try for a moment to recognize God at work
  in one of the difficult moments of your own life.
  Or ask God to help you see him there.

- Solomon is remembered especially for his wisdom.
  He himself valued this as a gift from God, more
  than riches or a long life. What image comes to
  mind when you think of a wise person? Can you
  recognize wisdom as a gift that you possess, or
  would want to possess, in any way?

Talk to the Lord

- Several times in the Gospels, Jesus is singled out
  as being a descendant of King David. He is born
  in Bethlehem because Joseph and Mary have to
  return to David's city for a census. Bartimaeus, a
  blind beggar, calls out to Jesus as "son of David."
  Yet Jesus is born in a stable and is executed as a trai-
  tor to the state. David is promised in the passage

that we have heard that he and his descendants will be kings over Israel forever. Matthew's Gospel believes that Jesus is a fulfillment of this promise. How do you react to the idea of King Jesus?

- As we come to the end of this time of prayer, speak to Jesus, called the "son of David" in Matthew's Gospel, about these ancestors of his and what their lives tell you about how God works in your life and the world around you.

Session 4
Invitation

- For today's exercise leading you into the stillness in which it becomes easier to hear the voice of God, spend a little time becoming conscious of the sensations of different parts of your own body. It doesn't matter whether you're sitting in a comfortable chair, lying down, or walking. First, be aware of the feeling of your feet, the shoes that surround them or the ground they press against.

- Then work your way up through your body—from your legs, your hips, your torso, your arms and hands, to your face and scalp. Let the feeling of each part register with you, and only move on when it has done so.

Stillness Exercise

- When you've reached your head, let your attention return to your feet, and move slowly again at your own pace through your body once or twice.

- Then, when you're ready, let that point of attention come to rest somewhere at the center of yourself. It's from that quiet center that you can now listen to the way in which King Jehoiachin was remembered by later generations.

Scripture
2 Kings 24:6, 8–15

So Jehoiakim slept with his ancestors; then his son Jehoiachin succeeded him.

Jehoiachin was eighteen years old when he began to reign; he reigned for three months in Jerusalem. His mother's name was Nehushta daughter of Elnathan of Jerusalem. He did what was evil in the sight of the LORD, just as his father had done.

At that time the servants of King Nebuchadnezzar of Babylon came up to Jerusalem, and the city was besieged. King Nebuchadnezzar of Babylon came to the city, while his servants were besieging it; King Jehoiachin of Judah gave himself up to the king of Babylon, himself, his mother, his servants, his officers, and his palace officials. The king of Babylon took him prisoner in the eighth year of his reign.

He carried off all the treasures of the house of the LORD, and the treasures of the king's house; he cut in pieces all the vessels of gold in the temple of the LORD, which King Solomon of Israel had made, all this as the LORD had foretold. He carried away all Jerusalem, all the officials, all the warriors, ten thousand captives, all the artisans and the smiths; no one remained, except the poorest people of the land. He carried away Jehoiachin to Babylon; the king's mother, the king's wives, his officials, and the elite of the land, he took into captivity from Jerusalem to Babylon.

Reflect

- In his account of Jesus' ancestry, Jehoiachin is the last name mentioned by Matthew before the Jewish elite are carried off to exile in Babylon. (Matthew's Gospel uses another version of his name: Jechoniah.) From what you have just heard, what first impression do you get of this unfortunate king?

- Historians would attribute the downfall of Jerusalem, recorded here, to the expansion of the empire of Babylon into the territory of its weaker neighbor. For the writer of this biblical narrative, the explanation is simpler. Jehoiachin "did what was evil in the sight of the Lord," and so he and his people were punished. Even without knowing the background, which of these explanations makes more sense to you here?

Talk to the Lord

- The theme of exile—to be without a homeland of your own, to be forced to live among strangers with different languages and different customs—has been an important one for the Jewish people from that day to the present. Jesus himself would have this experience when, shortly after his birth, he and his family had to flee into Egypt. Do you have any sense of what this feels like? You might draw on your own experience or that of present-day refugees you have seen on the news.

- Consider, too, the plight of those left behind. They are, the Scripture tells us, "the poorest people of the land." All their leaders, all the educated classes, even the army that was there to protect them, have been taken away. They are left as virtual slaves of the invading forces. Again, can you feel something of what this is like, perhaps drawing on stories you may have seen of trafficked people in our time?

- As this prayer draws to a close, you might perhaps want to speak to God for a few moments about present-day exiles and slaves, refugees and asylum-seekers. Or you might focus instead on what the idea of exile means in your own life. In either case, know that you will meet a God who reaches out powerfully to all those in need.

Session 5

Invitation

- As we begin this session of our retreat, start by becoming physically still. It doesn't matter whether you choose to stand up, sit comfortably, or lie down; just take up a position in which you can be, for a few minutes, both relaxed and alert. Stay quietly there for a few moments as you begin to relax.

- Now take time to notice what is going on inside yourself, in your mind and heart. What thoughts do you notice passing through your mind? What feelings are you aware of? As you take time to become more still, what do you find crowding your consciousness?

Stillness Exercise

- As you stay with these thoughts and feelings for a few moments, notice how these thoughts ebb and flow like a river. Some, perhaps, seem more important and long-lasting. Others are simply fleeting impressions that come and go quickly. For a little while, just continue to watch the movement of these thoughts and feelings as they pass through you.

- Try to detach yourself from these feelings even more. You aren't the swirling river of thoughts and emotions anymore; instead, you are watching the river from a distance, watching the thoughts and feelings. Spend some time peacefully observing all that is going on, without the need to get immediately involved. Let the river of thoughts and feelings continue on their journey. Meanwhile, from your quiet point overlooking the stream, listen to a passage from Luke's Gospel, describing an incident in the early life of John the Baptist.

Scripture
Luke 1:57–66

Now the time came for Elizabeth to give birth, and she bore a son. Her neighbors and relatives heard that the Lord had shown his great mercy to her, and they rejoiced with her.

On the eighth day they came to circumcise the child, and they were going to name him Zechariah after his father. But his mother said, "No; he is to be called John." They said to her, "None of your relatives has this name." Then they began motioning to his father to find out what name he wanted to give him. He asked for a writing tablet and wrote, "His name is John." And all of them were amazed. Immediately his mouth was opened and his tongue freed, and he began to speak, praising God. Fear came over all their neighbors, and all these things were talked about throughout the entire hill country of Judea. All who heard them pondered them and said, "What then will this child become?" For, indeed, the hand of the Lord was with him.

Reflect

- In this session of our Advent retreat, we look at three people who aren't in Matthew's list of the ancestors of Jesus. Zechariah, Elizabeth, and John aren't in the direct line that we have been tracing from Abraham onward. They are instead relatives, and contemporaries, of Jesus and his mother, Mary. Elizabeth had been thought to be incapable of having children. So the birth of her son is above all a cause of rejoicing for her and her friends and neighbors. Can you recall a time when you have shared the joy in the birth of a longed-for child?

- John will be the one who prepares people to receive Jesus. We're shown here God working powerfully from the first moment of his life. People react, we're told, with amazement and fear. Can you recall any time when you yourself have reacted to God, and to the work of God, with fear and amazement?

Talk to the Lord

- Names and the meaning of names are important to the biblical writers. Zechariah is insistent that his child should be called John, a name bestowed by the angel who told him that he would soon be a father. The name *John* means "God has been gracious." Can you apply that same idea, that God has indeed been gracious, to your own life? What evidence could you offer to support a claim like this?

- At the end of this passage, people are asking themselves, "What will this child become?" We know the rest of the story. He will baptize many, inviting them to turn away from their sins. He will recognize and make way for Jesus as one greater than he is. And he will fall afoul of a king by his preaching, and suffer a martyr's death in prison. What speaks to you most in the life and example of John the Baptist?

Session 6
Invitation

- As we've made our way through the different sessions of this retreat, you will have been led through a number of different ways of becoming more still and focused. You'll have drawn on the experience of your own breathing, of noticing the different sensations in your body, of calmly observing the ebb and flow of your thoughts and feelings. By concentrating on a physical object, you have been led into stillness, and by paying attention to the sounds around you, you've been able to discover an underlying silence within. Take a moment to recall some of these methods, and see if you can remember one of them that seemed to work well for you.

Stillness Exercise

- If you have found one of these techniques helpful, take a few moments now to lead yourself through it. Don't worry if you can't remember the details of how it was presented here; just let your own sense of how things work lead you deeper into stillness and silence. If you are new to these methods, you might prefer simply to sit quietly now and find whatever peace you can in all that surrounds you, as you prepare yourself to hear the Scripture passage that follows immediately after Matthew's list of the ancestors of Jesus.

Scripture
Matthew 1:18–24

Now the birth of Jesus the Messiah took place in this way. When his mother Mary had been engaged to Joseph, but before they lived together, she was found to be with child from the Holy Spirit. Her husband Joseph, being a righteous man and unwilling to expose her to public disgrace, planned to dismiss her quietly. But just when he had resolved to do this, an angel of the Lord appeared to him in a dream and said, "Joseph, son of David, do not be afraid to take Mary as your wife, for the child conceived in her is from the Holy Spirit. She will bear a son, and you are to name him Jesus, for he will save his people from their sins." All this took place to fulfill what had been spoken by the Lord through the prophet:

"Look, the virgin shall conceive and bear a son, and they shall name him Emmanuel," which means, "God is with us." When Joseph awoke from sleep, he did as the angel of the Lord commanded him; he took her as his wife.

Reflect

- In Matthew's eyes, this is the moment at which the work that God has been doing through the centuries comes to fruition. Now, take a moment to reflect on and appreciate the scope of God's work through all this length of time.

- It's clear from what is written here that the extraordinary circumstances of Jesus' conception and birth put Mary in a difficult position. She is pregnant before she is married, something carrying a huge social stigma in that society. And the explanation for all this isn't one that is going to be easily accepted by those around her. What must it have been like for her to have to bear this burden?

Talk to the Lord

- You are probably familiar with the story from Luke's Gospel of the archangel Gabriel being sent to Mary from God. In this account by Matthew, it is Joseph, not Mary, who receives the angel's explanation of what is happening and God's part in it. How do you see Joseph reacting to what he has been told? What does that tell you about the kind of man that he is?

- Jesus here is given the name *Emmanuel*, which means, we are told, "God is with us." A God who might otherwise seem remote and aloof has come to live right at the heart of his people. What does it mean to you to be able to say "God is with me, God is with us," in the context of your own daily life?

- Each year, as we celebrate Christmas, we recall these events. Speak to God for a few moments now about what this feast will mean to you this year, and whatever hope it evokes in you. Listen for whatever response God may want to offer you.

Enter into a Conversation with God

- In his book *The Spiritual Exercises*, Saint Ignatius of Loyola suggests simple ways to begin your prayer. "Consider," he suggests, "how it is that God our Lord looks at you." What's your first reaction to hearing this invitation?

- Jesus is God with a human face. It is literally possible, therefore, to imagine the look on Christ's face as he catches sight of you and then fixes his attention upon you. How would you describe that look to a friend who asked you about it?